Edinburgh

Edinburgh

Clive Hardy

Waterton Press Limited

First published in the United Kingdom in 1998 by
Frith Publishing an imprint of Waterton Press.

British Library Cataloguing in Publication Data.

Clive Hardy
Edinburgh

ISBN 1-84125-079-1

Reproductions of all the photographs in this book are
available as framed or mounted prints. For more information please contact The Francis Frith Collection at
the address below quoting the title of this book and the
page number and photograph number or title.

The Francis Frith Collection,
'Friths Barn', Teffont, Salisbury, Wiltshire, SP3 5QP
Tel: 01722 716376
E mail: bookprints@francisfrith.com
Web pages: www.francisfrith.com

Typeset in Bembo Semi Bold

Printed and bound in Great Britain by
WBC Limited, Bridgend, Glamorgan.

Contents

Francis Frith 1822-1898

Introduction
Francis Frith: A Victorian Pioneer

Francis Frith, the founder of the world famous photographic archive was a complex and multitudinous man. A devout Quaker and a highly successful and respected Victorian businessman he was also a flamboyant character.

By 1855 Frith had already established a wholesale grocery business in Liverpool and sold it for the astonishing sum of £200,000, equivalent of over £15,000,000 today. Now a multi-millionaire he was able to indulge in his irresistible desire to travel. As a child he had poured over books penned by early explorers, and his imagination had been stirred by family holidays to the sublime mountain regions of Wales and Scotland. "What a land of spirit-stirring and enriching scenes and places!" he had written. He was to return to these scenes of grandeur in later years to "recapture the thousands of vivid and tender memories", but with a very different purpose. Now in his thirties, and captivated by the new science of photography, Frith set out on a series of pioneering journeys to the Middle East, that occupied him from 1856 until 1860.

He took with him a specially-designed wicker carriage which acted as camera, dark-room and sleeping chamber. These far-flung journeys were full of intrigue and adventure. In his life story, written when he was sixty-three, Frith tells of being held captive by bandits, and fighting "an awful midnight battle to the very point of exhaustion and surrender with a deadly pack of hungry, wild dogs". He bargained for several weeks with a "mysterious priest" over a beautiful seven-volume illuminated Koran, which is now in the British Museum. Wearing full arab costume, Frith arrived at Akaba by camel seventy years before Lawrence of Arabia, where he encountered "desert princes and rival sheikhs, blazing with jewel-hilted swords".

During these extraordinary adventures he was assiduously exploring the desert regions of the Nile and recording the antiquities and people with his camera, Frith was the first photographer ever to travel beyond the sixth cataract. Africa, we must remember, was still the "Dark Continent", and Stanley and Livingstone's famous meeting was a decade into the future. The conditions for picture taking confound belief. He laboured for hours on end in his dark-room in the sweltering heat, while the volatile collodion chemicals fizzed dangerously in their trays. Often he was forced to work in tombs and caves where conditions were cooler.

Back in London he exhibited his photographs and was "rapturously cheered" by the Royal Society. His reputation as a photographer was made overnight. His photographs were issued in albums by James S. Virtue and William MacKenzie, and published simultaneously in London and New York. An eminent historian has likened their impact on the population of the time to that on our own generation of the first photographs taken on the surface of the moon.

Characteristically, Frith spotted the potential to create a new business as a specialist publisher of photographs. In 1860 he married Mary Ann Rosling and set out to photograph every city, town and village in Britain. For the next thirty years Frith travelled the country by train and by pony and trap, producing photographs that were keenly bought by the millions of Victorians who, because of the burgeoning rail network, were beginning to enjoy holidays and day trips to Britain's seaside resorts and beauty spots.

To meet the demand he gathered together a team of up to twelve photographers, and also published the work of independent artist-photographers of the reputation of Roger Fenton and Francis Bedford. Together with clerks and photographic printers he employed a substantial staff at his Reigate studios. To gain an understanding of the scale of Frith's business one only has to look at the catalogue issued by Frith & Co. in 1886. It runs to some 670 pages listing not only many thousands of views of the British Isles but also photographs of most major European countries, and China, Japan, the USA and Canada. By 1890 Frith had created the greatest specialist photographic publishing company in the world.

He died in 1898 at his villa in Cannes, his great project still growing. His sons, Eustace and Cyril, took over the task, and Frith & Co. continued in business for another seventy years, until by 1970 the archive contained over a third of a million pictures of 7,000 cities, towns and villages.

The photographic record he has left to us stands as a living monument to a remarkable and very special man.

Frith's dhow in Egypt *c.*1857

LINLITHGOW

Situated approximately half-way between Stirling and Edinburgh, Linlithgow became an important and favourite royal residence. During the wars with the English, the town and its castle were subject to siege and counter-siege. At Lent in 1314 the English took Linlithgow by blocking the fall of its portcullis with hay-cart. Edward II hurried through the town on his way to Dunbar and the safety of a ship, following his defeat at Bannockburn.

LINLITHGOW PALACE, 1897.   39155
The last Scottish national parliament was held here in 1646. Oliver Cromwell lived at the palace for several months following the Battle of Dunbar in September 1650.

PALACE FROM THE BOAT STATION, 1897.

King David I built the first manor house at Linlithgow, and next to it, the church of St Michael. In 1301, Edward Longshanks set about rebuilding and heavily fortifying the palace, and it was held by the English until the autumn of 1313.

THE RUINS OF LINLITHGOW PALACE ON THE SOUTH SHORE OF LINLITHGOW LOCH, 1897
Mary, Queen of Scots was born here in 1542, and Prince Charles Edward Stuart stayed here in 1745. The palace is thought to have been burnt down accidentally in 1746 by some of General Hawley's troops.

39154

THE QUADRANGLE OF LINLITHGOW PALACE, 1897. 39156
The Royal apartments were situated on the west side of the quadrangle. Queen Margaret's Bower is where her majesty kept vigil while James IV fought at Flodden.

ST MICHAEL'S CHURCH ADJOINING LINLITHGOW PALACE, 1897. 39158
Founded by David I in the twelfth century, the church was rebuilt about 300 years later.

THE CROSS WELL WITH ITS THIRTEEN WATER JETS, 1807. 39157
This well is a reconstruction of an earlier one destroyed by Oliver Cromwell's troops.

LINLITHGOW CHURCH, 1987. 39164a
On 23rd January 1570, Regent Moray was shot as he rode through Linlithgow. The assassin hid in a house belonging to John Hamilton, Archbishop of St Andrews. Moray's friends hanged Hamilton at Stirling in 1571. They did not go to the expense of a trial.

QUEENSFERRY

On the south shore of the Firth of Forth. South Queensferry and its counterpart North Queensferry are said have been so-named because Queen Margaret, crossed the Forth at this point on her way to Dunfermline.

FORTH BRIDGE, 1897

Designed by Sir John Fowler and Sir Benjamin Baker, the Forth Bridge cost £3,000,000 to build. Of the workforce of 4,500 men, 57 were killed in work-related accidents.

THE FORTH RAILWAY BRIDGE, *c.*1890.
Construction of the bridge commenced in November 1882. The first test trains ran from January 1890 and the official opening took place on 4th March 1890.

558

THE VIEW FROM NORTH QUEENS FERRY, 1897. 39144
The bridge is more than over 2,760 yards long, including approach viaducts, giving a clear headway at high water of 150 ft. The steel towers stand 360 ft high and are supported on granite piers. The deepest foundations are 88 ft below high water.

FORTH BRIDGE, 1897 ³⁹¹⁴¹

Following the opening of the Forth Bridge, the North British Railway Co., decided that they could dispense with their ferry services. Accordingly, the licences for the Forth and the Tay were transferred to David Wilson & Sons.

NEWHAVEN

This small fishing port was founded by James IV, in about 1500.
A shipyard and ropeworks were established for the construction
of warships.

HARBOUR, 1897   39139
The original population of Newhaven was probably of Dutch and/or Scandinavian origin. For generations the
people rarely moved out of their own community, keeping their traditions and customs alive.

View of Newhaven Harbour from Hawthornden, 1897. 39138

In about 1512 one of the biggest warships then in existence, was fitting out at Newhaven. She was The *Great Michael*, 240 ft long and carried a crew of 420 and 1,000 soldiers. The mighty warship was one of the units despatched by James IV to assist the French against Henry VIII.

FISHERMEN'S COTTAGES, NEWHAVEN, 1897.   39137
The fishermen's wives were known for their costumes which are thought to have had associations with the community's Scandinavian origins. The women also had their own cries when selling fish, 'Caller Herrin' (fresh herrings) and 'Caller Ou' (fresh oysters).

EDINBURGH

Edinburgh became Scotland's capital without ceremony more than 500 years ago when James II decided to hold his parliament in the town. Edinburgh (Old Town) was quite small, consisting of only a few hundred houses huddled in close proximity to the eastern side of the Castle. Just when Edinburgh was founded is open to speculation. The name is thought to be a derivation of 'Edwin's burgh', Edwin being an early seventh century king of Northumbria. At the time Northumbria was all powerful. Its territory extended from the Forth to the Humber, and Edwin is known to have fortified a part of the area occupied by the present castle. Edwin also encouraged a civilian settlement nearby. Under David I, Edinburgh was a royal burgh, which brought with it a number of trading privileges. In David's day, Church and State were interlinked and it was David who re-introduced monasticism back into Scotland. David granted tracts of land and gave vast amounts of money to the greater glory of God, encouraging Benedictines, Cistercians and, most of all Augustinians, to found religious houses. The legend goes that David was out hunting when he was attacked by an infuriated stag, he was then saved from certain death by the interposition of a miraculous cross. In thanks, and as a penance for hunting on a holy day, David founded an abbey at Holyrood.

Despite the foundation of a great abbey, much of Edinburgh's early history appears to revolve around the castle and the fortunes of the monarchy. Henry VIII was desperate for his son Edward, aged five, to be married to the infant Queen Mary. Scotland at that time was under the governorship of James, 2nd Earl of Arran who was a Protestant. Through argument, coercion, and downright bribery, Arran persuaded the Scottish parliament to agree to the match, and it was ratified in two treaties at Holyrood in August 1543. But Scotland, as so often in the past, was in turmoil. Mary of Guise, the infant Queen's mother, was against the wedding and had the backing of a number of nobles and the Catholic Church. For some reason, Arran suddenly changed faiths and sides and the infant was crowned Queen of the Scots, Henry was not impressed. In May 1544 an English invasion force arrived off Newhaven. Edinburgh fell to the troops of the Earl of Hertford, though the castle managed to hold out. Hertford burnt Holyroodhouse and the Old Town.

The following year Hertford was back in Scotland, burning five market towns, sacking 243 villages, and laying waste to crops. Edward was destined not to marry the Queen of Scots. He died in July 1553 and was succeeded by his Catholic sister. The young Scottish queen was married to Francois, Dauphin of France, an act that was to establish the Auld Alliance. The marriage lasted two years. By 1560 Francois too was dead and Mary had returned to Scotland.

HOLYROOD PALACE AND ARTHUR'S SEAT, 1897. 39168
Extensive alterations to the palace were undertaken between 1670 and 1679 by Sir William Bruce, the king's Surveyor in Scotland. The strong French influence in Sir William's designs reflected Charles II's passion for things Gallic.

KING CHARLES'S BEDROOM INSIDE HOLYROOD PALACE, 1897. 39172
A fence and rope guard the old feathered four-poster bed, with the once, elaborate canopy and drapes, giving the bed a majestic air.

INSIDE HOLYROOD PALACE, 1897. 39173
Another corner of King Charles's bedroom. The worn looking armchair and bed canopy have seen better days.

FRONT ENTRANCE, HOLYROOD PALACE, 1897. 39169
The building of Holyroodhouse was started in about 1500 by James IV, the work continuing under James V who added a new tower and quadrangle. In May 1544, the palace was badly damaged when it was set on fire by the Earl of Hertford's troops.

CHAPEL FRONT, HOLYROOD HOUSE, 1897. 39170
The Chapel Royal at Holyroodhouse. It originally the nave of an abbey founded in 1128 by David I.

THE REMAINS OF THE CHAPEL ROYAL AT HOLYROODHOUSE, 1897. 39171
The burial place of David II, James II and James V, the chapel was sacked during the revolution of 1688. The real damage was done in 1768 when the roof collapsed.

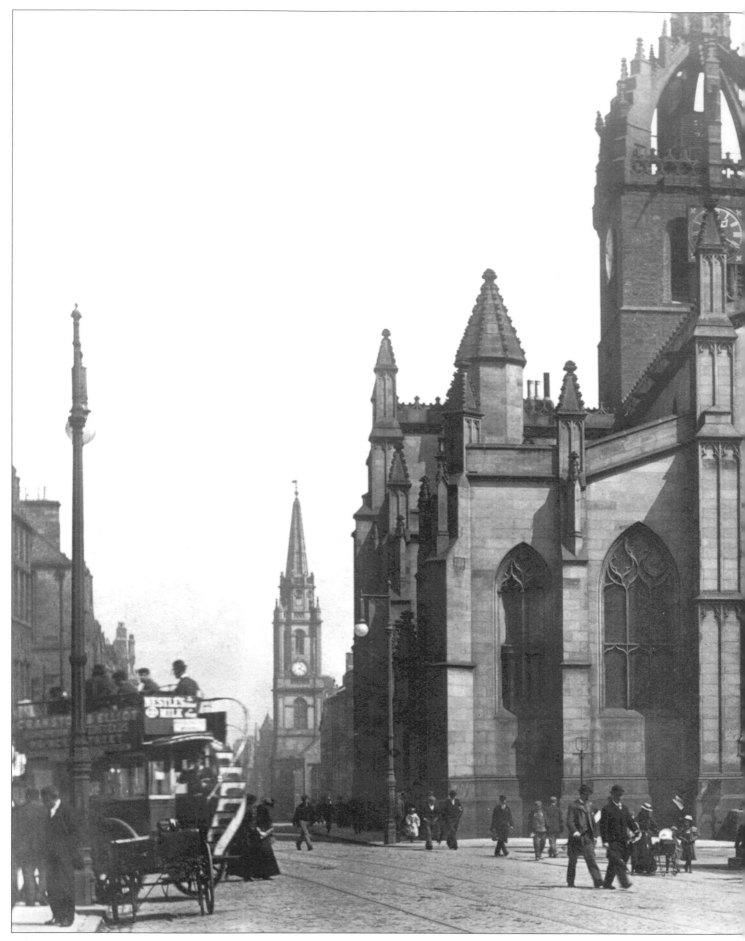

ST GILES' CATHEDRAL, 1897.
The High Kirk of St Giles was largely built in the fourteenth and fifteenth centuries. The tower, which dates from *c.*1495, is topped off with what is considered to be the finest example of a crown steeple in the whole of Scotland.

HOLYROODHOUSE AND THE DOMINATING MASS OF ARTHUR'S SEAT.
At 822 ft high, the seat stands in a 648 acre park.

E24502

THE CANONGATE TOLBOOTH, *c.*1883.   E24503

The Canongate was where the canons of Holyrood Abbey entered the Old Town. The tolbooth, with its projecting clock, is one of the most famous landmarks on the Royal Mile and dates from 1591.

CANONGATE STREET, 1897.   39124A

In the great days of the Old Town, Canongate Street was where members of the Scottish aristocracy had their town houses.

JOHN KNOX'S HOUSE, 1897. 39125
The lower reach of the High Street looking towards Canongate. The building immediately behind the lamp standard is known as John Knox's house. Dating from the sixteenth century, the house is said to have been built by Mary, Queen of Scots' goldsmith. Just how long Knox lived here is open to debate.

St Giles' Cathedral, 1897.

39127

In 1634, Charles I attempted to re-establish the Scottish Episcopal Church and St Giles's was for a short period elevated to the status of a cathedral. Again under Charles II, St Giles's became a cathedral only to revert to being a parish church in 1688.

St Giles' Cathedral, 1897.

39129

The oldest parish church in Edinburgh, it was erected in the early twelfth century on the site of an older building. In 1385, much of the church was badly damaged by fire, and the rebuilding was not completed until 1460.

St Giles' Cathedral, 1897. 39128

St Giles's in 1897. During the Reformation, the interior of the church was defaced; altars and relics were destroyed. In 1559, John Knox was appointed minister of St Giles's but the building was in fact divided into four separate churches and remained so until the nineteenth century.

THE TOMB OF THE GREAT MARQUIS OF MONTROSE, 1897.

In 1644, James Graham, 5th Earl of Montrose, raised an army to fight for King Charles I. Against all odds, Montrose gained victory after victory until his luck finally ran out at Philliphaugh in September 1645. Montrose escaped to the Continent but returned to raise troops for Charles II. Betrayed to the Covenanters, he was hung, drawn and quartered at Edinburgh on 21st May 1650.

A BATTALION OF THE BLACK WATCH ON THE CASTLE ESPLANADE, 1897.
Raised by General Wade in 1725, the Black Watch was formally constituted as a regiment of the line in 1739, its strength being increased from four to ten companies.

39121A

CASTLE FROM THE GRASSMARKET, 1883.
The grassmarket was the scene in 1736 of the Porteous Riots. A temporary gallows had been erected for the execution of Andrew Wilson for smuggling. Captain 'Black Jock' Porteous was in command of the city guard that took Wilson to his execution. A disturbance broke out and Porteous ordered his men to open fire on the crowd. He was later arrested, tried and condemned to death but because of the circumstances of the case, a stay of execution was granted until the king returned from Hanover. There were many people in Edinburgh who hated Porteous and, fearing that he would be pardoned, a mob broke into the jail, hauled him off to the Grassmarket and lynched him. Despite the offering of a large reward for information, no one was ever charged with Porteous's murder.

E24303

THE CASTLE FROM JOHNSTON TERRACE, 1897.   39120

During the reign of James III, the king's brothers were imprisoned here on suspicion of conspiring against him. John, Earl of Mar, died in Craigmillar Castle after being over-bled whilst suffering from a fever. Alexander, Duke of Albany, managed to kill his gaolers and escaped down a rope made of sheets.

THE CANNON 'MONS MEG', c.1950.   E24001

The cannon *Mons Meg,* is said to have been cast at Mons, Belgium in 1486, on the orders of James III. When James IV came to use the brute at the siege of Norham Castle in 1497, it took an artillery train of 220 men and 90 horses to get *Mons Meg* to the scene of the action.

CASTLE AND NATIONAL GALLERY, 1897.
The Edinburgh Castle we see today is, with a few additions, that built by the Earl of Morton following the siege of 1572. Morton succeeded Lennox as Regent and took the fortress in the name of the infant James VI from the supporters of Mary, Queen of Scots. It was Morton who added the great half-moon battery to the castle's defences.

E24506

CASTLE FROM THE GRASSMARKET, 1887. 39121
The site of the Marquis of Montrose's execution was not here but at the Mercat Cross in the High Street. Having been declared a traitor in 1644, Montrose was not given the benefit of a trial. After hanging for three hours, his body was taken down and quartered. His head was set upon the tolbooth, his limbs sent for public display on the gates of Stirling, Glasgow, Perth and Aberdeen. In 1661, Montrose was allowed a state burial.

THE CASTLE FROM PRINCES GARDENS, 1897. [39119]
The gardens, railway line and Princes Street occupy the area once covered by the waters of Nor' Loch. The loch and an area of marshland formed a part of the castle's defences but also inhibited Edinburgh's expansion. The decision was taken in the 1770s to drain the loch and marshland to allow the development of the New Town.

A VIEW FROM THE CASTLE, 1897.
In the foreground are the buildings of the Royal Institute and the National Gallery, with Princes Street on the left behind the Scott Monument. Carlton Hill can be seen in the distance.

A TRAMCAR RATTLES OVER THE JUNCTION OF FREDERICK STREET AND PRINCES STREET, 1950.
Edinburgh was well served by its tramway system for 85 years, services coming to an end in November 1956.

E24003

EDINBURGH UNIVERSITY, 1897   39134

Edinburgh University was founded by James VI in 1582. The buildings in this picture were constructed between 1789 and 1827, the dome being added in 1887. By the early years of the twentieth century, the University had 3,000 students with 40 professors, 43 lecturers and 44 examiners.

A VIEW FROM THE CASTLE, c.1950.
A similar view to as on pages 44–45, but separated in time by 50 years.

E24004

HERIOT'S HOSPITAL, 1897. 39135
George Heriot, goldsmith and banker to James VI, founded the hospital. He was immortalised as Jingling Geordie in Walter Scott's Fortunes of Nigel.
Construction began on the hospital in 1628 but it was not completed until 1693 when it saw service as a military hospital.

EDINBURGH INFIRMARY, 1897. 39133

Built in the Scottish Baronial style, at a cost of £400,000, the infirmary was dealing with 8,000 patients a year by 1900.

DONALDSON'S HOSPITAL, 1897. 39136

It was erected and endowed for the maintenance and education of up to 300 children of whom 100 had speech and/or hearing difficulties. The benefactor was a wealthy printer who died in 1880, leaving £200,000 for the project.

THE ROYAL INSTITUTION AT THE FOOT OF THE MOUND, 1897.
Founded in 1823 the building housed a statue gallery when this picture was taken. There was also a collection of casts that was open only to art students.

39115

39106

NATIONAL GALLERY, 1897.
The collection included paintings of the Spanish and Italian Schools and the British were represented by artists such as Gainsborough. The annual Exhibition of the Scottish Academy was one of the highlights of the year.

PRINCES STREET LOOKING WEST, 1897.

It was possible to keep healthy on Princes Street. The Edinburgh Cafe at number 70 did not serve alcohol and there was a Turkish baths at number 90. For those with a sweet tooth, Edinburgh rock was available at Ferguson's.

WATERLOO PLACE, 1897.

In the background on Carlton Hill stands the unfinished monument to the Scottish dead of the Napoleonic Wars. The monument was started in 1822 but the money ran out and it was never completed.

THE ROYAL INSTITUTION, 1897.
The magnificant entrance to the Royal Instituion in 1897.

EDINBURGH FROM CARLTON HILL, 1897. 39103A

In the foreground is the castellated bulk of the prison. The old Carlton burial ground just beyond is where the philosopher David Hume is buried.

SCOTT MEMORIAL, 1897.
A view of the Scott Memorial, in the foreground a nanny enjoys a well earned rest.

WATERLOO PLACE, 1897.
On the left is the Register House containing the Scottish archives. Over on the right is the general post office. The statue is of the Duke of Wellington.

PRINCES STREET, 1897.
39112A
Note the cabs and brakes alongside the Scott Monument. During the summer, excursions could be taken from here to the Forth Bridge and Queensferry and also to Roslin.

PRINCES STREET AND SCOTT MONUMENT, *c*.1900. E24504
Princes Street and the Scott Monument from another part of the gardens.

PRINCES STREET LOOKING EAST, 1883. E24301
The interesting thing about this picture is the road traffic, which seems to be keeping to the right-hand side of the road. This might have something to do with the fact that omnibuses, brakes and cabs often parked alongside the Scott Monument on the left.

PRINCES STREET, 1897.
At the turn of the twentieth century Princes Street boasted a number of hotels. The most expensive to stay at
was the North British at Waverley Station. Next on the list were the Caledonian Station and the Royal,
followed by the somewhat cheaper Royal British, the Douglas and the Bedford. There was also the Old
Waverley, which was a temperance establishment.

39108

THE SCOTT MONUMENT AND PRINCES STREET GARDENS, *c.*1900. E24510

The monument was designed by George Kemp and built between 1840 and 1844. Scott owned several houses in the city, the most famous being 39 Castle Street, where he wrote many of the Waverley novels.

PRINCES STREET WEST END, 1897.

Considered to be one of the finest boulevards in Europe, Princes Street was the place to shop and eat. Restaurants included a branch of Ferguson & Forrester, the Royal British, and Littlejohn's. Confectioners included Mackies, and Ritchies where shortbread was a speciality.

39113

Princes Street, 1897.
The junction of Hope Street, Queensferry Street and Sandwick Street in 1897. St John's and St Cuthbert's Churches, along with the castle, provide the backdrop.

39114

WAVERLEY STATION, 1833.   E24302

The platform canopies were still under construction when this ture was taken. The station was originally called North Bridge but was renamed in April 1866.

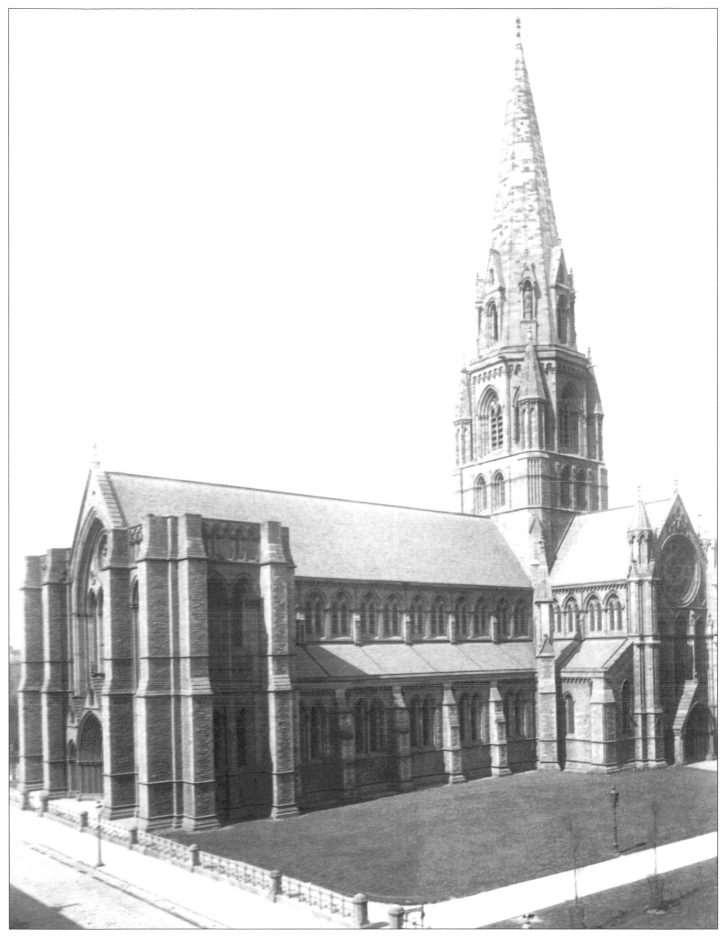

ST MARY'S CATHEDRAL, 1897.
Designed by Sir Gilbert Scott, construction began in 1874 and was finally completed in 1917.

PRINCES GARDENS, 1897.   39122
Prince Gardens in 1897 looking towards The Mound.

ST MARY'S CATHEDRAL, 1897. 39132
The imposing interior of St Mary's Cathedral. By 1879, construction costs amounted to more than £110,000.

ROSLIN

Roslin is famous for its castle and chapel. The oldest part of the castle, which was founded by Sir William Sinclair, dates from the early fourteenth century. The consecration of the chapel was delayed because a murder had been committed on the premises by the chief stone mason.

CASTLE FROM THE GLEN, 1897.

39167

The castle stands on a cliff above the river North Esk. The oldest part dates from the early fourteenth century. It was enlarged in the 1440s.

ROSLIN CHAPEL, 1897. 39164
The chapel famed for its elaborate carvings, was founded in 1446 as a collegiate church, but only the lady chapel and choir were completed. The church was badly damaged by rioters in 1688 and was restored in the nineteenth century.

ROSLIN CASTLE, 1897.
All but destroyed in 1544, during an English invasion, the castle was rebuilt by 1580. Further additions were made during the seventeenth century.

39166

ROSLIN CHAPEL INTERIOR, 1897.
The chapel is famed for its pillar of entwined ribbands. The story is that the chief stone mason went to Italy to study a similar pillar. While he was away his apprentice worked out how to construct the pillar after having a dream and built it. On his return, the mason was so jealous of his apprentice's work that he struck the boy dead.

PART OF THE OLD RUINS OF ROSLIN CASTLE, 1897.   39165
The castle and church have long been popular with tourists, many of whom stay to sample the delight of the Old Rosslyn Inn. Among those to imbibe have been Johnson and Boswell in 1773, Robert Burns, Queen Victoria and Edward VII.

HAWTHORNDEN

Located nine miles south of Edinburgh, Hawthornden stands high above the river North Esk amid a densley wooded estate. The home of the poet William Drummond (1585-1649), the house was extensively rebuilt by him in 1638.

HAWTHORNDEN, 1897.   39159
The English poet laureate Ben Jonson stayed here from December 1618 until the middle of January 1619 as a guest of William Drummond.

THE COURTYARD AT HAWTHORNDEN, 1897. 39163

Jonson was 45 years old when, in 1618 he left London and walked the 400 miles to Scotland. At Darlington his shoes gave out and he had to buy another pair. He later told Drummond that they took some breaking in and left his feet sore and blistered for several days.

HAWTHORNDEN FROM THE GLEN, 1897.
A picturesque view of Hawthornden.

BEN JONSON'S TREE, HAWTHORNDEN, 1897.
It is said that Drummond was sitting under the great sycamore tree in front of the house when Jonson trudged up the path. Drummond met him with 'Welcome, welcome royal Ben!' Jonson replied 'Thank ye, thank ye, Hawthornden!'

39162

39160

HAWTHORNDEN FROM THE GLEN, 1897.
Drummond's library was one of the finest of its day, containing about 1,400 books in English, French, Latin, Greek, Spanish, Italian and Hebrew.

86

NORTH BERWICK

It was at North Berwick, in 1591, that the devil is said to have appeared to a group of witches in St Andrew's Kirk. At their trial for witchcraft, the women confessed that they not only knew the most intimate secrets of the king's bedchamber, but that their satanic leader was none other than Francis Stewart, Earl of Bothwell. Bothwell, though well educated was probably mad and not afraid of using violence. The king, who believed in witchcraft, ordered Bothwell's arrest. Bothwell escaped from custody and crossed into England, only to return at Christmas and attack Holyroodhouse, threatening to torch the place. It was almost certainly the intervention of some of the local citizens that saved the situation from getting completely out of hand. An attempt by Bothwell to kidnap James was botched but, not to be outdone, the earl descended once more upon Holyroodhouse, demanding a trial for witchcraft. Bothwell never got his trial. He left Scotland and eventually died in poverty at Naples.

NORTH BERWICK, 1897. 39183
Tourism brought with it a spate of hotel building. The Royal was joined by the impressive Marine Hotel which had hot and cold running water.

QUALITY STREET, NORTH BERWICK, 1897.
The corner shop is long gone but the clock tower remains.

39176

THE LAW, 1897.   39175
North Berwick Law rises 612 ft above the town. On the summit is a watch-tower dating from the Napoleonic Wars, and an archway made from the jawbones of a whale.

MARINE HOTEL AND LINKS, 1897.
North Berwick's popularity as a resort began in the 1840s but, as late as 1859, when HRH The Prince of Wales visited the town, there was a serious lack of accommodation for tourists. The project to build a hotel somehow became involved with plans for a new gas works under the North Berwick Hotel & Gas Company.

THE SEAFRONT, 1897.
The popular seafront of North Berwick.

NORTH BERWICK BAY, 1897.
The broad sweep of the sandy bay to the east of the harbour area on a quiet day in 1897.

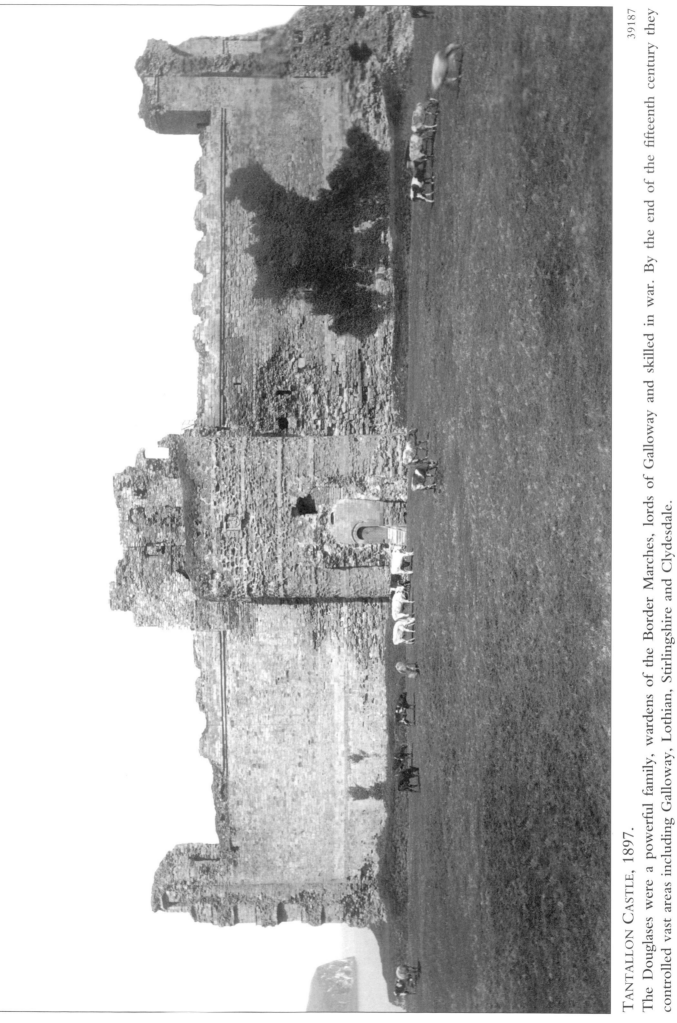

TANTALLON CASTLE, 1897. 39187
The Douglases were a powerful family, wardens of the Border Marches, lords of Galloway and skilled in war. By the end of the fifteenth century they controlled vast areas including Galloway, Lothian, Stirlingshire and Clydesdale.

TANTALLON CASTLE, 1897. 39184

In 1388, the 2nd Earl of Douglas invaded the Earl of Northumberland's domain to the south. Douglas raided far and wide then after capturing Northumberland's standard, returned home. On 5th August 1388, the two sides clashed yet again. In the savage hand-to-hand fighting that went on all night Douglas was killed and the Earl of Northumberland was taken prisoner.

THE BASS ROCK, 1897. 39188

One of the more interesting events in the history of this famous bird sanctuary occurred after the Battle of Killicrankie in July 1689. Despite defeating the forces of William III, the Jacobites failed to hold the advantage. One of the outcomes was that the Bass Rock was taken and held in the name of James VII from June 1691 to April 1694.

TANTALLON CASTLE, 1897.
James V was resentful of the Douglas', so he laid siege to Tantallon in 1528. Red Douglas held out for three weeks before surrendering. Douglas went into exile in England and his estates were forfeited to the crown.

39186

LADIES WALK, 1897.   39181
The finely wooded grounds of Tyninghame House, the seat of the Earl of Haddington, the grounds were open to the public on Saturdays.

WHITEKIRK

The village and church probably owe their existence to the discovery of a holy well in 1294. Aeneas Sylvius Piccolominic (later Pope Pius II) came here during the reign of James I.

THE VILLAGE, *c.*1955.
A view of the village of Whitekirk.

W3275002

St Mary's Church, *c.*1955

The fifteenth century cruciform church of St Mary's, its massive tower is surmounted by a wooden spire. The church was targetted by the suffragettes during a campaign of violence following the government's refusal to grant votes for women. Other targets for fire-bombing included Farrington Hall and Leuchars railway station.

BLACKBURN

Sandwiched between Whitburn and Livingston, Blackburn in West Lothian stands on the River Almond. This selection of pictures were taken at the beginning of the 1960s.

THE CENTRE, *c.*1960S.   B7585008
A bleak featureless view of Blackburn New Town.

The Centre and Bowling Green, c.1960s
Typical 1960s structures span the whole photograph. This was the typical layout of a 1960s 'new town.

RIVER ALMOND AND HOPEFIELD BRIDGE, *c.*1960.
The River Almond flows into the Firth of Forth at Cramond. A prophetess at Cramond is said to have warned James I of impending tragedy if he continued with his journey to Perth. He was murdered.

BLACKBURN SHOPPING CENTRE AND THE GOLDEN HIND HOTEL, c.1960.
The precinct is typical of a style that dominated redevelopment and new town schemes of the late 1950s and 1960s. Examples can be seen throughout the UK, many of them now looking the worse for wear.

B7585004

THE ALMONDVALE 'OLD FOLKS' HOME, c.1960s   B7585002

Again a typical 1960s structure. Everything looks unused in this photograph, the 'Old folks' home looks unlived in as yet, and the trees seem to have been just planted.

THE LIBRARY, c.1960s   B7578007

This forbading structure was Blackburns 'new town', library. The rotunda structure in the foreground was probably used as a reading room.

RIVER ALMOND, *c.*1960.
The River Almond flows from Blackburn to the three towns of East, Mid and West Calder. It was at Mid Calder in 1556 that John Knox first administered Communion according to Protestant rites.

B7585005

Themed Poster Books £4.99

000-7	Canals and Waterways	
001-5	High Days and Holidays	
003-1	Lakes and Rivers	
004-x	Piers	
005-8	Railways	
044-9	Ships	
002-3	Stone Circles & Ancient Monuments	
007-4	Tramcars	

Town & City Series £9.99

010-4	Brighton & Hove	
015-5	Canterbury	
012-0	Glasgow & Clydeside	
011-2	Manchester	
040-6	York	

Town & City series Poster Books £5.99

018-x	Around Brighton	
023-6	Canterbury	
043-0	Derby	
020-1	Glasgow	
011-2	Manchester	
041-4	York	

County Series £9.99

024-4	Derbyshire	
028-7	Kent	
029-5	Lake District	
031-7	Leicestershire	
026-0	London	
027-9	Norfolk	
030-9	Sussex	
025-2	Yorkshire	

County Series Poster Books £4.99

032-5	Derbyshire	
036-8	Kent	
037-6	Lake District	
039-2	Leicestershire	
034-1	London	
035-x	Norfolk	
038-4	Sussex	
033-3	Yorkshire	

ailable
oon

County Series £9.99

045-7	Berkshire	
053-8	Buckinghamshire	
055-4	East Anglia	
077-5	Greater London	
051-1	Lancashire	
047-3	Staffordshire	
049-x	Warwickshire	
063-5	West Yorkshire	

County Series Poster Books £4.99

046-5	Berkshire	
054-6	Buckinghamshire	
056-2	East Anglia	
078-3	Greater London	
052-x	Lancashire	
048-1	Staffordshire	
050-3	Warwickshire	
064-3	West Yorkshire	

Country Series £9.99

075-9	Ireland	
071-6	North Wales	
069-4	South Wales	
073-2	Scotland	

Country Series Poster Books £4.99

076-7	Ireland	
072-4	North Wales	
070-8	South Wales	
074-0	Scotland	

A selection of our 1999 programme:
County Series and Poster Books
Devon, Cornwall, Essex,
Nottinghamshire, Cheshire.

Town and City Series and Poster Books
Bradford, Edinburgh, Liverpool, Nottingham,
Stamford, Bristol, Dublin,
Stratford-upon-Avon, Bath, Lincoln,
Cambridge, Oxford, Matlock, Norwich.

Themed Poster Books
Castles, Fishing, Cricket, Bridges, Cinemas,
The Military, Cars.